I0467174

Marketing Analytics Mastery: From Strategy To Application

SADANAND PUJARI

Published by SADANAND PUJARI, 2024.

Table of Contents

Copyright

Copyright © 2024 by **SADANAND PUJARI**

Marketing Analytics Mastery: From Strategy To Application

Master The Fundamentals Of Marketing Analytics And Start Measuring The Impact Of Your Marketing Efforts Like A Pro!

First Edition: Jun 2024

Book Design by **SADANAND PUJARI**

About

Feeling overwhelmed with your marketing data? You're not alone! 83% of marketers say they struggle "to adapt to the volume of data" created by their marketing efforts, while 80% feel that there are "too many performance metrics" to keep track of. Today, it's essential for everyone to possess a foundation in data literacy. Whether you're an analyst, a brand manager, creative, or even a CMO, understanding how to collect, interpret and action your marketing data is quickly becoming the standard, rather than the exception.

I designed this Book based on more than 10 years of knowledge and experience working directly in the field of data analytics and market research. We'll cover everything from theory to application, to ensure you're equipped with the knowledge to make sense of your marketing data and make logical, data-driven decisions both quickly and consistently.

I am pretty confident that the Book will give you the necessary knowledge and skills to immediately see practical benefits in your workplace. Go ahead and click the enroll button.

Introduction

Hi and welcome to this marketing and ethics Book on data mining customer lifetime value. If you are a marketing manager looking for a big business or an entrepreneur owning a business you would understand how important it is to find out customer lifetime value companies which spend more on customer acquisition than then determining which customer to date. Very quickly go out of business Moreover investors and V.C. firms often value the business base as the number of customers you have and the average lifetime value of your customers in this Book. You will learn how customer valuation is done analytically. Firstly we will use concepts of net present value and customer John to predict the lifetime value of a set of customers.

This will also be able to evaluate the effectiveness of our promotional campaign. Secondly, we will model highly uncertain situations using Monte Carlo simulation which will enable you to estimate the range of outcomes of your marketing decisions. All the concepts dart intuitively will be implemented in excel. So we will be considering business scenarios and solving them in Microsoft Excel. You will be learning practical concepts on these techniques which are actually used by consulting firms and marketing and index funds. This is a small Book and I'm pretty sure that you will be able to complete it once you start so let's start and see you in the next chapter.

Lifetime Customer Value - Key concepts

In this chapter, we will learn what his customers value and why it is important. You may have seen offers like this on sites like Groupon nearby or any other coupon website which offer discount coupons. In this example snapshot, you can see some bizarre companies offering their pizza for $10 when its retail prices are $20. That is they are putting it at a discount price of 50 percent. Oftentimes, the cost of making a pizza, maybe even more than $10, while a discounted price is less than $10. That is the ultimate prize. Maybe less than the cost. This goes against the intuitive idea of selling a product at more than the cost of that product. It may seem that if we follow this strategy, eventually we are going to suffer from heavy losses.

So why is this strategy popular and why do so many dealers offer such discounts? The concept behind this is the customer's lifetime value. The idea is that even if a customer is giving $10 and not covering the cost of the product, eventually customers will order again or even in this order. Customers will buy something else from the shop, eventually leading to a higher customer margin or profit. So instead of giving importance to the instantaneous value of a transaction, we give importance to long term value generated by a customer. So in this chapter, we are going to learn how to calculate this long term value of a customer so that we can cite appropriate discount prices to acquire the customer.

To calculate customers lifetime value, there are two terms which are very important that we should understand before we start calculating lifetime value. The terms are discount rate and retention rate. Discount rate refers to the interest rate. Do not confuse it with the discount that you are offering on that product. It is a generic term which is often used in financial analysis or discounted cash flow analysis. It means that the value of money that you have today is more than the value of the same amount of money that you will have in the future. So if you have one dollar today, that is worth more than one dollar one year from now. Why is that so? So if you have one dollar today, you can invest it in the stock market, you can put it into a bank savings account.

Or by security bonds with it. And after one year, it will give you one plus some interest amount. This interest will be the best country that we will consider in our calculations. So for example, if you have one dollar today. And the discount rate is 10 percent. Then that $1 is the same as one point one dollar up to one year. So the present value of one point one dollar after one year is $1 to the. So then we are trying to estimate customers' present value and will first estimate the revenue that customer is going to generate in the coming years. And then we will discount that value using the discount rate. To find the net present value, if a customer is giving us ten dollars after one year, we will divide that 10 by one point one if the discount rate is 10 percent, if the discount rate is 20 percent, we will divide it by one point two. So this is how we will use the discount rate to find the net present value.

The second term is retention rate. This is the percentage of customers that are retained over a given period of time by retaining women that these customers will do a repeat purchase. Opposite of pretension is John, or appreciate. That is the attrition rate or churn rate will be one minus retention. So if we are retaining 60 percent of the customers, that is 60 percent of the customers buy from our store again after their first purchase. We have a retention rate of 60 percent, which is the same as John Reid's 40 percent attrition rate of 40 percent. This distinction is calculated over a period of time, so we usually take a period of one year, so a retention rate of 60 percent will mean that over one year.

If we had a hundred customers at the beginning of the year, we would have only 60 customers at the end of the year, 40 of those customers, the journal. I will not do any repeat purchases. To clarify these concepts, let us look at this example, suppose at the start of year one, we have 100 customers, we have a discount rate of 10 percent. And the retention rate of 80 percent. The profit per customer. We are generating 10 units. Given this information, if I want to find out the present value, this is how I do it. For the past year, I have had 100 customers. Profit, but customers didn't. So I multiply 100 with 10 to get a revenue of 1000 directly. If we ignore the cost for now, this revenue is the same as profit for us.

Since this revenue is generated at the beginning of year one, the present value of this housing unit is told annually. Now we move on to year two. 80 percent of our customers. Do repeat parties 20 percent. Never business to know our customer base is only 80. Profit, but customers then so we generate a revenue of 800. This note will be generated at the beginning of year two. So we will be getting this eight hundred units of money after one year, so the present value of this eight hundred units of money is eight hundred divided by one plus 10%. So eight hundred divided by one point one comes out to be seven twenty seven point two. So. In year three, we further have 80 percent retention, so 80 percent of it is 64.

Revenue is 64, 60 210 640. Not this 6:40 we get after two years, that is the beginning of year three. So we have to discount it twice when we divide 640 by 1.1. We get the value of 640 at the start of second year. We are going to divide this value by one point to get the present value of the 640 units of money. So we get 640 divided by one point, one used to power two, which comes out to fight. Do you really need some money? We continue whether we. Have a retention rate of 80 percent, which gives us nearly 51 one customers. Fifty one multiplied by 10 gives us a venue, if I wonder, can we divide by 10, by one point one three times? So one point one is to what three? That gives us a value, theoretically, we continue doing this.

Bill, we have zero customers. We had all the net present value for all these years to get the total present value of this business. When we divide this total present value of the business by the number of customers that we have, initially, we get the lifetime value of customers. I hope you understand the concept in the next chapter, we will be implementing these concepts in Microsoft Excel. So even if you have some doubt by looking at the Excel sheet, your doubts will be clear. If you still have any doubts, you can ask them in the discussion.

This is a milestone!

First of all, I want to congratulate you for starting this Book. You may not know this, but out of all the enrolled students, only 20 percent reached this point. So you are already in the top 20 percent of the students. We hope that you continue the same energy and motivation throughout the Book and complete the school's students like you inspire us to create a five star Book by motivating us to continuously upgrade the Book, add additional resources and answer your queries. I also want to give you some information about the review system.

Edit your reading option. If you face any technical issues like chapter bloody or audio muting, you can change the chapter player setting from here. If the problem persists, you can contact the technical support of your enemy. All of our letters have gone through the extensive quality check of your enemy, and I assure you that there is no technical problem with any of our chapters.

You can also enable English subtitles using this button to help you through this Book. Apart from this, if you have any coast related queries or suggestions, you can reach out to us through direct messages or Q&A portal. For a direct message, go to our starting academy profile. And click on the send message button. For Q&A. Just go to the Q&A tab and ask a question, and I will personally solve all your doubts and questions for readers on our teaching skills and content. It would be better if you can write a review along with the star reading. Once again, congratulations, you are already among the top 20 percent students of the schools. Keep up the good work and complete the scores.

Remember what Mahatma Gandhi told us about learning to live as if you were to die tomorrow and learn as if you were to live forever.

Lifetime Customer Value - Excel model

Then this Excel sheet, we will learn how to find out. Net present value or the customer lifetime value. But indeed, this country and indeed. You can see I have two cells in the top of the sheet. Discount rate, attention, attention. You can change the values that I have included here. These are sample values for your business, you've been tainted attention and discount rate as part of your business. Now I'm going to do this analysis on a yearly basis. So the first column contains. Twenty is one, two, three up to 20 years. The initial set of customers I'm going to use in this example is 100. Some of these customers will turn out after the first year. Which I'm going to calculate it as indeed it intended. So what do I have the number of customers in even multiplied by the retention rate? So these customers are retained by the ad business.

I have 60 customers, so I want to extend this formula to other states. Before doing that, I have to turn on the 60 faucets, so then I drag it down. Deceitful, who remain as people see it should increase that it could become C nine, C 10 and so on. We know the solution. So in C nine, I have seen it in the sequel. I drag it down to the next cell. I haven't seen 90 sequels. This is what I want to achieve. I put dollars in both in front of the sea for self-defense. No, I double click on the bottom right corner of this cell so that I get all the values for only 20 rows. You can see that for the bottom few rows devalues nearly zero. So we could have done a cutoff at 50 cents after that, we have nearly zero customers.

But it hardly makes sense after 50, the number of customers is nearly zero, and we then multiplied the number of customers that profit per customer. It is still going to come out when you lose you. So it will not impact the net present value. Third column is the profit margin per customer. This is basically the revenue generated by a customer, minus the total costs incurred on acquiring that customer, plus production cost of that one unit gold plus other marketing expenses and so on. So this affects the margin. Revenue minus all the costs in the port column, I will be giving you the margin total margin is product, the number of customers that we have. Margin, but customer. So the first year I am getting a total profit margin of polling units, double click on the bottom right corner.

Look, total profit margin for the coming years. The last column in this table is the present day value as it relates to that value. Didn't discount this country. In the first year. We considered this new. Of the thousand units, Hooters' thousand units of margin was donated at the beginning of this year. So the net present value of this thousand units of money is basically we divide this total margin with one plus discount rate raised to the power. Here's the value minus one. When we do this, it is one one minus one becomes zero. Then I put one plus discount rate to dip over zero. This dump becomes one. The denominator becomes one. So this present value comes out to be one thousand divided by one, which is one.

Not to extend it down. I'll put all those animals in front of these sea trees, said the shortcut of putting daughters in windows. You select that reference and you. Press Airport. Now, let's examine this akin to. Not the numerator is the total margin of this. This 600 units would indicate at the beginning of second year, so it is up to one year. We divide with one plus these concrete ways to resolve it here. Value minus one values two minus one. So you get one. Since we are getting this value after one year, we raise the one plus discount rate to deposit one. This value comes out to be. They fortified. I extend this formula to all the other rules. This is the present value of all the margin generated by all these customers. If I add this predictive value of all these years.

I get the bottle within the value for customers if I want to find out the customer lifetime value. I will divide this value by the number of customers, which is one. So the customer lifetime value is coming out to be going to units. What does this lifetime value of two units of money mean? As you can see. The margin per customer was only 10 units. That is considered an example, suppose you're selling a visa. For $20 and the cost places $10. So the margin we're debating. But, Peter, assuming that the customer is ordering only one visitor thing, so the margin you're generating per customer is $10. Suppose they offer this piece up at a price point of five dollars. This is a web discount opening my visa at a discount of 75 percent, the market value was a million dollars.

Now I am offering it at $5. Well, suppose this $5 B is getting me 100 customers. But these are not customers, I'm incurring a loss of $5 200, which is $500. So when I launched this, I incurred a loss of $500 and might gain 100 customers. But these new customers over the next 20 years are going to generate so much margin. For weeks, if I calculate a deep total present value, it comes out to be two thousand two hundred dollars. This means giving five hundred dollars, three. I am the new head of a new $2200. So although the date may not seem logical, but. Or Peter Pan? These are new customers, I'm going to give you so much value that this deal will eventually be profitable for you. This is how businesses use customer lifetime value concepts to offer.

Attractive deals to acquire new customers. Now, in this example, I assume that the revenues generated at the beginning of the year, which means that this thousand years of margin was acquired at the beginning of the year one. Some names in some subscription models, this thousand dollars would be generated at the end of the. Which means that you have to find the present value of this thousand dollars too. So depending on when this happens. Cash flow is going to be generated in the beginning of the year in the middle of the year or the end of the year. You need to get the corresponding value of this cash flow. There is a formula in Excel, look at net present value. It assumes that the cash flow is being depleted at the end of the.

So this housing value that I will give it as a barometer, it will continue to be generated at the end of the year. Let's find out the NPV. So using the formula in BP, which stands for net present value, I input the discount rate as the first, but I'm on the market parameter and it calculates the net present value of these given sets of values. Note that it takes the assumption that these margins were generated at the end of the year, not at the beginning of the year. You can see that there is a difference of nearly $200 between net present value if the gas goes up in the beginning of the year versus the value if cash closes at the end of the. That's all in this.

Sensitivity Analysis in Excel

In the last chapter we learned how to calculate customer lifetime value. By creating this day, the two most important parameters that we used were discount rate and retention rate. It is very important that the impact of changing the values of these two parameters on the customer lifetime value. In practical scenarios, the discount rate, that is, business government policies, central bank policies and market situations retention rate often varies based on the retention effort that you provide the customer experience and customer service that you provide. So it is important that we see the sensitivity of customer value with these two parameters. This sensitivity will tell me how robust my model is if the customer value does not change much by changing discount rate and retention rate. Then we have a fairly robust customer value card loaded with us.

If it is changing a lot with a small change in discount rate and retention rate. Firstly we need to calculate very precisely what is the actual discount rate and retention rate Secondly by doing small changes in these two things. We can significantly improve our profit and customer lifetime value so it is important that we see what is this sensitivity of lifetime value against these two parameters. One simple way to estimate the effect of changing values of these two parameters is to actually change the value of the parameter in these cells. So here it is 10 percent. If I make it twelve percent you can see that net present value changes to twenty one hundred fifty three which was earlier twenty two hundred nearly.

This is simple but it will be tedious if we want to take it for a number of combinations of these two values. To handle that efficiently we use a functionality called data table of Excel for this. We first create our tabular structure of the different values of these two parameters. So in this row I have a discount rate of 10 percent. We have already calculated the present value. I have put 20 percent 14 percent and 16 percent as the other values to be tested in this column. I have retained a 60 percent value but we do not know the outcome. The retention rate is 60 percent but the discount rate is 12 percent or 14 percent similarly. We will check what the impact of having retention rate is 70 percent, 80 percent or 90 percent. You can change these sets of values as per your business requirement.

Once you have created this data table in this intersection sale of the table we need to input the formula which is to be used to calculate the value in all these sales. Since we already calculated the net present value in each cell by writing the whole formula in Edgerton we are just going to rate it equal to it. It hit No. Select the complete table. Go to data and underwater for analysis. Select Data table the raw input is this discount rate so we will select C to resell column input is the retention rate so we will select DC for sale what will happen is for each value in this data stable in this row that is 10 percent 20 percent 14 percent 16 percent all these four values will be put in this row input that is DC 3 sell this column which contains data intended these 60 percent 70 percent 80 percent 90.

percent all these what values will report one by one in this sea for sale when these two combination of values are put her the NPV will be calculated and it will be stored in the corresponding sale then I'll click okay it generates the whole beta table you can see that the fossil is giving the same value which we had initially for 60 percent and 10 percent what same discount rate if I increase retention rate by 10 percent my net present value increases immensely by nearly 600 units which is nearly 30 percent of the initial value and if I go horizontally that is if I increase discount rate by 2 percent my net present value decreases by a small amount nearly 50.

unit this highlight that the retention rate is a very important parameter like calculating customer lifetime value a small effort towards retaining customer will generate a very high margin in terms of customer value so this is all we create a data table the use of data table is finding all the customer value in different scenarios one reason of doing that is when we present our business to investors or to business managers we often called the optimistic and the pessimistic value of this customer acquisition marketing activity so in this scenario when there is 14 percent discount rate and 60 percent retention rate this may be taken as a pessimistic estimate of customer lifetime value and a discount rate of 10 percent with a retention rate of 80 percent maybe taken as an optimistic number for customer lifetime value. So in this way using data tables we generate different scenarios and find the customer lifetime value in all these different scenarios.

Variations in finding customer value

So till now we have seen how to calculate customer lifetime value using retention rate discount rate and a constant customer margin over a given set of years. Now in practical scenarios there may be some variations to this simple model in our model. We assume that we are getting all the revenue at the beginning of the year. That is our customers. All of them are paying us at the beginning of the year. It may not be true that the customers may be over the year, they may be paying at the end of the year or maybe somewhere in the middle. We have to take into account that some of these customers may turn out in that period of time.

That is if the customers are paying in the middle of the year some of the customers that we had in the starting of the year may leave our business in the middle of the year when the time to pay comes so we have to use the retention rate to find the number of people at the time of payment only these customers will be paying. And only that much amount will be taken as a new so. If we have some X percentage of retention rate, if you are generating revenue in the beginning, all hundred percent of the customers will be giving us the revenue. If we are generating revenue at the end of the year, a hundred percent retention rate will be churning out till the end of the year.

So hundred into a retention rate only. That many people will be retained till the end of the year and only they will be paying for our services in the third scenario. If the customers that are in the middle of the year or debt payments are uniformly distributed over the year you can consider taking the average of customers you have in the beginning of the year and customers you have in the end of the year to have corrected that one minus retention rate here. So basically this is the number of customers who will be paying at the end of the year. And these are the number of customers who will be paying if we are getting revenue in the middle of the year or dipping into distribution uniformly over the year.

So here's an example. If we have a hundred customers and the retention rate is 80 percent. If we get all the money in the beginning we can consider all the hundred customers to be paying. If we get revenue at the end of the year we should take only 80 customers. That is 80 percent off and if we get revenue in the middle of the year we have to take the average of hundred and eighty to get this value of 90. So this is one variation where you have to consider when your revenue is being generated and you have to consider how many people will be paying for their business. According to that model similar is the case with discount rate.

If your revenues are being generated in the beginning of the year such as the case that we discussed in the Excel sheet we just need to find out the net present value for the previous year so in the first year when you will get the revenue you do not need to do any discounting but if your revenues are being generated at the end of the year for the first year revenues also you have to discount that by dividing it with the discount rate so if your revenues are generated at the end of the year you have to discount it by a factor of one by one plus this country in the beginning of the year you have a factor of 1. In The middle of the year we will have half of it.

So it is one divided by one point. To devour half this value of one point one is being used because we have considered that we have a discount rate of 10 percent. This is a value you can change in your Excel sheet. As we discussed in the last chapter, according to our example if these revenues are generated in the beginning you do not need to do any changes or that is we just multiply that profit with one and do the normal NPV calculation process if it is entered in the end. We divide all the profits by one point and then do the normal NPV process if it is needed in the middle.

We divide all the profits by one point one days to about point five and then do the normal NPV calculation process last prediction that we are going to discuss is the changing value of margin over the period of pain so it is not necessary that a customer who is using our service will keep on giving you the same profit margin over its lifecycle a loyal customer maybe giving you higher profit margins or eventually if your services are getting degraded the customers may start giving you lower margins so if you remember in that excel sheet in this column we consider constant margins and that is a customer is giving us 10 units of profit margin every year. If this value is changing you have to take into account that also and you have to change the values here.

So if you expect that the margins will keep on increasing at some particular rate you increase the margin here but that rate till the end of the customer lifecycle and how will you find out whether the margin will change for the customer or not. You can do a secondary search, you can do competitor analysis, you can do primary research that is to go and talk to your customers and so on. So identify whether the customer margin will change or not if it will not. You can use this model if you change the values of margin in this column and then run the NPV model to find the customer value. So these are some of the variations that we wanted to discuss in this customer valuation topic.

Monte Carlo Simulation - Introduction

In this chapter we're going to learn how to use Monte Carlo simulation to find out. Customer value a lot of real life problems are very complicated and not plagued with uncertainty. There are numerous events that could happen and it is very difficult for a marketing analyst to calculate the probability of a particular event happening and to find out the corresponding benefit or loss. In such situations where there is a lot of uncertainty Monte Carlo simulation is one method which can help us predict the outcome or at least give us the expected outcome of different scenarios. So in this chapter I'll show you a simple example to first make you understand what Monte Carlo simulation is then in the coming chapters will take up a business case.

We will discuss that business case and try to solve that case in Microsoft Excel too. As I told you Monte Carlo simulation handled scenarios of uncertainty here is a very simple scenario. When I want to find out if two days are true, what is the probability of getting a sum equal to seven? So if I get a two and a five THIS I MAY 7 I want to find out what is the probability of getting some as 7 now. There are two ways to find out this probability. One is mathematical in mathematical delusion. We look at the probability distribution of dice and try to mathematically calculate the probability we will see how to do that. The second solution is we can actually rule these days a large number of times and find the ratio of how many times we actually get the sum as 7 so we can roll the dice.

Ten thousand times if we get the sum of seven one hundred things there is a 1 percent probability of getting some as 7 so these are the two options. Let us explore the first option. Look at this diagram in this we can see all the different scenarios that can happen when I throw two dice. The first idea is I get one and one which is a sum of two take internet users sum of three which is done in two ways then a sum of four which can be done in three ways sum of five. And lastly some of which is only possible if I have six and six on board erase all these scenarios. If you count it comes out to be 36 so the probability of getting some as to is this one chance out of 36 or getting some three is these two chances out of 36. So to buy 36.

My question was: What is the probability of getting a sum of seven, that is, these six scenarios divided by the total number of variables, which is 36. So six by 36 is equal to nearly sixteen point seven percent. So this is how we calculate the mathematical solution. We can also write any formulas to get to the same result. The second option as I told you earlier is to simulate this scenario. That is we will actually rule two days and then paint and we will see the outcome of how many times we actually get a sum of seven and we will use this ratio as the probability of this event happening. So the event of actually doing these days can be simulated using software.

That is we can generate a random number between 1 to 6 with an equal probability of any number. Coming up this can be said to be an electronic dice so we will use Microsoft Excel in the next chapter to generate two random numbers between 16 we will do this 10000 banks and we will see these some of these two randomly generated numbers and we will see the number of paint the sum of these two randomly generated numbers is 7.

Monte Carlo Simulation - Example

So in this chapter we are going to simulate the event of twin two days and then we will try to find out what is the probability of getting some of seven minutes or to raise so here I have created ten thousand cases and for each case will be generating two random numbers. So four dice one we will generate a random number using the line between function and this random number should be between 1 and 6 similarly for days to. We will again generate a random number between 16. We will select these two. Click on the bottom right corner to extend this to all the other cells in this table. Now in the sport column I'll be finding out the sum of the value in these two days.

You can see every time I perform any action on this sheet the line between function refreshes. So the random number generator in the second and third column will be deflation. Every time you perform any action in this worksheet. So now the problem statement is how many times do we get some s seven. You can see for the first case I am actually getting somewhere seven again in the twenty third case. These are my seven. So I want to find out out of these 10000 cases. How many sevens are in default column support that we will use. Counting function will come from this set of values whenever the value matches seven so you can see in 10000 observations nearly seventeen hundred observations have the same as seven you'll find out this ratio.

Seven seventeen hundred fourteen divided by 10000 so it refreshed and now I'm getting a percentage value of nearly 16 percent. If you can remember in the last chapter when we calculated it using mathematics it was coming out to be sixteen point seven percent. If I refresh it every day so you can see that we are roughly getting the same number. This is the concept behind Monte Carlo simulation. We will generate many scenarios and we will see the outcome of those scenarios then we will find out the ratio of favorable outcomes upon total number of outcomes. To find out the probability of that favorable outcome happening this is in histogram which I just plotted to show you that this shape is similar to the shape that we saw in the last chapter when we actually mathematically calculated the probability for different cases.

So for some of us we had a very low probability then it increases for sum of three sum of four and it goes to the maximum for some is equal to seven. Then it again starts to decrease and it is the minimum for something. So this was a simple example in which we could easily calculate the probability using mathematics also. And we easily model it using Monte Carlo simulation but a lot of real life problems have so many variables and so much uncertainty that mathematically solving it becomes very tedious and very difficult. In such a scenario using Excel we can model those situations and run those scenarios for a large number of aims and correspondingly find the probability doing this by hand would have been very difficult. But since we can use software, this Monte Carlo simulation method is popular to find probabilities in very complex situations. In the next chapter we will discuss a business scenario which we will solve. Using Microsoft exit.

Problem Statement

In this chapter we will discuss a business scenario in which we can use more big ideas in relation to find out the customer value. Consider this scenario. Lisa works as a marketing manager in ecard. She's asking for the help because you have done a Book on marketing analytics, so she's saying that ecard sends out promotional emails to all the customers every month. If a customer does not buy any product for 24 consecutive periods twenty four consecutive months they will stop sending the email. She has also shared the cost of my profit policy in a different Excel sheet. This excel sheet we will see in something. Also she has looked at the past data to identify the probability of whether a customer will buy or not buy the product.

Depending on how recently that customer transacted with us and how many transactions that customer has done with us. So how recently the transaction is captured in the DNC and the number of transactions with the customer is captured in frequency. These are these two values. She has found out the probability that a customer will buy or not buy business. Previous data now she is asking your help to optimize this promotional campaign. So let us go and check out the excel file.

Monte Carlo Simulation in Excel: Part 1

So here is the excel sheet shared by Lisa with us and this sheet. You can see the probability of whether a customer is going to buy based on the frequency and the decency value that is. Consider this frosted for a customer who has bought in the last month. That is the decency is one and that customer is bought only once that is. Frequency is one if we send this customer a mail to buy a new product. There is a ten point three percent chance that this customer is going to buy that product. If you go horizontally forward, that is if you keep recency as one it is giving you the probability for all those customers who bought in the last month but in their lifetime they have made more than one purchases from our company.

If you go vertically down the frequency of transaction will remain the same. That is the customer has bought only ones from us. The reason he's changing that is that customers may have bought two months back, three months back or even 24 months back. As we mentioned, after 24 months of inactivity we will remove that customer from our mailing list. I'll take a few minutes to explain how Lisa could have created this day but to create this table Lisa would have used historical data. So for all the customers of the company she sent out a mail to buy a new product. Some customers belong to this category. That is the DNC is one fragrances one. Some customers belong to this other category decency to frequency one and so on.

So she sent out a message to all these customers who might need them whether they actually bought or they did not. Then she found out the ratio of how many in each category bought against the total number of customers in that category. So when she sent out mail if there were a thousand customers belonging to this category one hundred three out of them actually bought the product and others did not. So that is why she is saying that there is a probability of ten point three percent of a customer buying the product belonging to this category. So I hope you understand our recency and frequency table. The first step of running a Monte Carlo simulation in this scenario is creating this day with other information that is shared is that the cost per meal is one unit and sales revenue generator policy is 60 units.

You can change this data as your company's scenario. I will discuss these other three values when we reach a point where we are going to use these three values. So this is the scenario. This is the business problem. Now it is time to solve it so as you know we are going to solve this using Monte Carlo simulation. We will simulate the scenario for one customer in this table. The output of that one customer will be simulated 10000 times in the second they will when we run it 10000 times. We will find out the average outcome that is average customer value for different scenarios from this second debate. So let us first create this table for one single customer. These are all the things that we are going to end.

The first column is period. This is the period for which we send out the promotional mail. So since we were considering monthly mails. So this is about a month. The number of periods we are going to consider is 80 because we expect our customers' life cycle to be nearly six-seven years. The next column is whether that customer is still going to get mail from us or not. The J cares if that customer has not bought anything from us in the previous 24 periods we will stop sending the email. So if we will not be sending anything into a default period we will start writing no here.

Otherwise this value will be yes then this is the value of recency. I have equated this to the sale which is the initial recency as I told you this scenario is for one particular customer for this customer. Assuming that the initial decency and frequency values are one and one later on then we will simulate for 10000 customers. We will be changing the decency value from 1 to 24 because the customer when we are sending the mail could belong to any great degree with licensee rating from 1 to 24 frequency. We are going to keep it as one only. This is to signify that we are considering only those customers who have purchased from us only once.

That is we are trying to simulate the situation only for our new customers. The next column is the probability that buying this column will get the value from the table above the decency and frequency table so corresponding to the decency value and the frequency value in the previous two columns. We will get what the probability of that particular customer buying is. Next we will look at the last column. This is the random number we are generating. We will generate a random number between 0 and 1 using the line function and the line function generates an equally likely number between 0 and 1. This is where we are going to capture the randomness of our scenarios.

So for this particular customer when we send out the mail in the first period the probability of buying is going to be nearly ten point three percent. We will generate a random number if that random number is less than zero point 1 0 3. Then we will see that particular customer will buy. I hope you see what we are trying to do here. We are trying to simulate a customer buying with a probability of ten point three percent. We generate a random number and we check if that random number is less than ten point three percent. We say that the customer will buy if it is more than ten point three percent. We will say that customers will not buy and the probability of this number being less than ten point three percent is actually ten point three percent so we will generate a random number in this column.

We will compare if this random number is less than the probability of buying. If it is, we will say the customer will buy. So a yes will come here. If it is no then if it is more than this probably we will say no here every time we send a mail we will add a cost of 1 revenue generation will also come from this table. If the value in this by the mail is yes we will add revenue. If we were not able to sell we would not add this sales revenue. Total profit is going to be revenue minus cost. We will calculate total profit for all the 80s period. Once we have this column failed we will find the net present value of all this revenue generated using the concept of net present value or the customer value discounted at a fixed rate. We are going to use 3 percent.

Monte Carlo Simulation in Excel: Part 2

So let us fill this first role. The probability of buying will come from that upper table. So in this end we want to find out what is the probability of buying given the recency and frequency values for this. We are going to use the INDEX function. The first thing we need to check is whether we are going to send the mail or not. We will first put in a function. We will check if the mail is going. If this is not going on. If there is not going then the probability is due. If it is going then we will go to the upper table. And we will use this index function. The first parameter in this index function is the table values which are from these six to eight twenty nine. The second parameter is Ronan. Ronan is the recency value.

And the third parameter is column name column name is frequency value. So by telling index function the table boundaries and the random and the column name that we want to find out the value for we will get the probability of buying since we will be extending this formula to other sales also we will put dollar symbols in these cells which we do not want to change when we drag this formula down to other cells. So you can see that I am getting this value of ten point ten point three percent which is the same as this. First see if I just change the frequency well to do this it is automatically updated and I am getting this twelve point one percent value next I'll put the AND function to get a random number than it did between 0 and 1. This is a random number generated between 0 and 1.

I'm going to put a condition in this column that if this randomly generated number is less than probability of buying then the value should be yes. If this randomly generated number is less then this probability of buying then yes or 1 and 0. So you can see a randomly generated number as point seven which is more than point 1. So it is showing me zero. If it was less than point 1 this by value would be 1 no cost is the cost of sending this mail as long as we are sending demand we will be cutting the cost so we will just take if devaluing still going column this value is yes then we will take the cost as given in this table. Else the cost will be zero. We will put dollars in build for this key to a decision also. Because when we extend this, say , extend this formula to other cells we do not want the reference of this bill to be changed.

Net contribution from sale is the revenue that we are going to generate. If we sell. So if the value in my column is 1 then we will generate revenue on the table above that is 60. It will generate zero revenue again. Will put dollars and build on this difference in total profit is going to be revenue minus cost thus zero minus 1 now for the recency and frequency columns we need to change these values. If the customer buys or does not buy whenever a customer buys the decency value for the next period will become one because the customer would have recently bought our product. And whenever the customer buys the frequency value will also increase by 1. If the customer had bought our product three times and the customer buys it one more time the frequency will increase from three to four.

So recency will be reset to 1. Every time a customer base and frequency will be increased by one every time a customer base in case of nobody's that is customer does not buy a product. The recency will increase by one not as if a live customer bought 3 months ago and the customer did not buy it. This time also in the next time period the customer would not have bought our products for the last four time periods meaning early meaning a recency value for frequency value will not change in us an idea of no way. So we will write those two formalizing recency and frequency table indecency. We will say that decency is if last month by value is zero recency is going to increase by 1.

So last time it was 1 this month is going to be two other ways recency is going to be reset to 1 for the frequency column relate. If the last month by value is zero, frequency remains the same as last month. Is it increased by 1 now? For this column in which we were checking whether email is going to be sent or not. We said that the rule is if the customer does not buy it for twenty four consecutive periods we will stop sending emails to that customer. So if a customer is not buying for 24 consecutive periods that means that the recency value would be 24. So if the recency value is more than 24 then the value would be no. Otherwise it will be yes. So let us complete the second rule by extending the formula to the second row. Then we will select all of this second row and we will extend it to complete detail.

You can see for this customer the by column stays zero. That is this is one of those unlucky customers for those that never buys a product. The random generated number is always greater than the bipolarity value. And unfortunately this customer never buys and after the 24th period we stop sending the emails to our customer. So this customer costs US one dollar twenty four times and generates no revenue and this sale of total customer value. We will find out the net present value using the NPV function. The discount rate is prettyThe final milestone! And this is the array of values so when I entered this formula the probability values refreshed and this customer has now bought the product two times. So for this particular customer who buys our product two times the customer value we are getting is thirty two dollars.

Had it been the earlier customer who never bought up this value would have come out to be some negative value. So this is simulating this scenario for just one customer. Now we are going to simulate it 10000 times for 10000 customers. Also since all these customers could belong to any decency value, that customer could have bought our product five months ago. Customers could have bought our product 10 months ago. So we are going to consider all those 24 scenarios also in which recency value will vary from one to 24.

Conclusion

So in this table I have created 10000 rules and 24 columns. Now we are going to use the data table functionality of excel in the data table functionality we use. We are going to use this table that we have created with 10000 rows and 24 columns in the top most left and the top left corner. We are going to use it. We are going to specify the formula which is to be used to calculate the value so when I equated this cell to this cell it gave me an error of incorrect reference. I clicked on the small l prompt and clicked on three sets of it told me that the error starts from here. The error is coming here because this function in this cell included an index in the index.

We wanted to find out the probability corresponding to this recency and this frequency value recently is one frequency to six. When Excel tried to find that particular combination recency is one but there is no corresponding value for frequency of six. It is due to this issue that we are getting a reference error here. So we are going to handle this by adding additional. So here we are going to take an additional assumption. The assumption is going to be that if the frequency value is more than five we will use the same probability values as we were getting for frequency is equal to fight so we'll add an additional function which will check if frequency value is greater than 5.

It will change that frequency value to 5 so now I am getting the customer value and the top left corner of this data table. So we will select this whole table first to select the complete table. You can use the shortcut of control plus shift plus low key so to select all the columns go to the fossil press control shift. Radke then to select all rows. Press control shift donkey now. Once I have selected the data table I'll go to the Data menu select water for analysis click on the table here I'll tell what the raw inputs in the raw input cell is the cell in which the values will be changed from the raw of this table. So the row of this table has values one, two , three , four and so on till 24 for recency.

So we will change the recency value in this initial recency say to have selected this all in the column inputs then we will select any random blank cell in which Excel will randomly put these values we will randomly select any blanks in these 1 to 10000 values will be randomly will be one by one put into that blank cell we are selecting a blank sin because because this value is nowhere use in our calculation recently when it was used from this table. But this simulation value is not used. So we have selected any random blanks and I click Okay. So here is the output of our data table for the first customer.

If the recency value was one the expected customer value was 40 units what the second customer expected value was minus 16 unite our customer also. Fourth customer until fifth customer gave a very high customer value of one hundred one unit and so on. So we have this for 10000 such customers. Similarly for customers with a recency value of 2, recency value of 3 and so on. Let us find out the average customer value of each group so in this way I'll find. Average of all the values in this column so for these 10000 customers with recency value of 1 the mean customer value is coming out to be thirty point seven three units so customers with recency value of 1. If you continue to send emails to them in their lifetime on an average.

Such customers will give you a value of 30 units. Let us extend this for other categories also. So if you look at the average customer value for all these categories in the last few categories the customer value is nearly zero or even negative. That is, emailing such customers is not generating profit but it is generating loss. So our idea that we will keep on sending emails till the customer has shown no activity for 24 consecutive periods is flawed. It will lead to some loss to us. It would make more sense if we stop sending emails after the customer has shown inactivity for 18 periods. So still this period we are getting customer value off more than one. You can still sell for these categories but the value you're going to get is very small.

But for this set of customers with very low recency values it is definitely a very good proposition to send out these promotional mails since these are going to give us a lot of business. You can see how by stimulating the deal to avoid a scenario of uncertainty for one customer and then simulating it for a lot of customers. We simulated it here for 10000 customers. You could do it for even a hundred thousand customers although it may take a lot of pain but it is doable and correspondingly we saw the returns. When we simulate this for a lot of customers when we look at the returns we can draw important inferences that invade scenarios. We are going to get profit and in return we are going to incur losses.

We also learned from this example that different categories of customers give us different customer value. So when we are calculating total customer value or our business value we need to consider different types of customer segments and calculate customer value accordingly. Here we model a third entity based on recency and frequency. There could be uncertainty in terms of other variables also. Probably you have different stores and different stores give out different probability of sales, different types of email to give or different probability of sales so there could be different scenarios in which there will be different types of untoward entities. All those you can model it using previous data you can create a probability distribution using that probability distribution. You can simulate it for a number of times and find out the profit and loss scenarios. That is all in this chapter. Thanks.